CONTENTS

THE STORY SO FAR...

When *The X Factor* judges put Perrie, Jesy, Leigh-Anne and Jade together as a brand new girl group they had no idea how big Little Mix would become.

HOW IT ALL BEGAN

The group's story started way before *The X Factor*, back when Little Mix hadn't been thought of, before the girls had even met each other. In Romford, South Shields and High Wycombe four strangers shared the same dream – to sing and perform.

But for Jesy, Perrie, Jade and Leigh-Anne fame seemed out of reach. 'Normal' girls like them didn't become popstars. Luckily, with encouragement from their friends and family, the girls worked hard towards achieving their dreams and never gave up, even when things got tough.

Then, one day in 2011, fate brought the four hopefuls together. As soon as the girls became a group, things just clicked. They worked hard, they found their voice and an unbreakable friendship blossomed.

When they made history by becoming the first group to win *The X Factor*, the next chapter of the girls' lives began. Giving interviews, recording songs, touring and being on telly became the new 'normal'.

Fans went wild for the foursome, loving their quirky style, upbeat songs and undeniable friendship. Little Mix mania had begun.

LITTLE MIX TIMELINE

1991
The Nelson family celebrate the arrival of Jessica on 14th June. Leigh-Anne Pinnock arrives four months later on 4th October.

1992
Jade Thirlwall is born on 26th December.

1993
On the 10th July, a matter of miles from baby Jade, Perrie Edwards is born.

2008
A nervous Jade auditions for *The X Factor*. She gets a 'yes' from the judges and makes it as far as Boot Camp.

2010
Jade auditions for *The X Factor* again but is gutted to be sent home from Boot Camp once more.

2011
In different parts of the UK, the girls all audition as soloists for *The X Factor*. They all get through to the next stage but the judges aren't really sure where each girl fits. At the end of Boot Camp they're put into a group together and are amazed to make it through to the Live Shows.

As Little Mix the girls impress the judges and the voters becoming the first-ever band to win the competition. Their debut single, *Cannonball*, goes straight to number 1.

2012
Still riding on an *X Factor* high, the girls get their second chart-topper when *Wings*, a song written to inspire young fans, is released in September.

Their first album, *DNA*, comes out in December and peaks at number 3.

2013
Missy Elliott features on the single *How Ya Doin'?* which comes out in April. *Salute*, Little Mix's second album with a more R&B sound, is released in November and reaches number 4 in the album charts.

2015
The girls top the charts again in July when *Black Magic* goes straight in at number 1. It's a busy year with four more singles being released. The album, *Get Weird*, comes out in November with a more mature sound. It peaks at number 2.

2016
Little Mix prove they've still got it *when Shout Out to my Ex* becomes their fourth number 1 in October. The girls get an early Christmas present when *Glory Days* becomes their first number one album, in December.

2017
In February, the girls win their first Brit Award when *Shout Out to my Ex* gets Best British Single. A month later, the band releases *No More Sad Songs* featuring superstar rapper Machine Gun Kelly. The cheeky video is set in a country and western bar and shows the girls sporting cowboy hats, line dancing and riding bucking broncos.

The future...

WATCH THIS SPACE!

FACT FILE

FULL NAME:
Perrie Edwards

BIRTHDAY:
10th July, 1993

STAR SIGN:
Cancer

FROM:
South Shields

STYLE:
Vintage/boho

FAVOURITE SHOP:
Topshop or Urban Outfitters

LIFE BEFORE FAME:
Student

MUSIC ICON:
Beyoncé

FUN FACT

Perrie used to do an Amy Winehouse tribute act complete with wig!

PERRIE

FACT FILE

FULL NAME:
Leigh-Anne Pinnock

BIRTHDAY:
4th October, 1991

STAR SIGN:
Libra

FROM:
High Wycombe

STYLE:
High fashion

FAVOURITE SHOP:
River Island

LIFE BEFORE FAME:
Waitress

MUSIC ICON:
Rihanna

FUN FACT

Leigh-Anne has no sense of time so is always running late!

LEIGH-ANNE

FACT FILE

FULL NAME:
Jade Thirlwall

BIRTHDAY:
26th December, 1992

STAR SIGN:
Capricorn

FROM:
South Shields

STYLE:
Boyish/geeky/cute

FAVOURITE SHOP:
Zara

LIFE BEFORE FAME:
Student

MUSIC ICON:
Diana Ross

FUN FACT

Jade's North East accent is so strong that when Jesy first met her she couldn't understand a word Jade was saying!

JADE

FACT FILE

FULL NAME:
Jessica Nelson

BIRTHDAY:
14th June, 1991

STAR SIGN:
Gemini

FROM:
Romford

STYLE:
Street/rocky

FAVOURITE SHOP:
Topshop

LIFE BEFORE FAME:
Worked in a bar

MUSIC ICON:
Missy Elliott

FUN FACT

Jesy is obsessed with trainers and owns about 400 pairs!

JESY

GET PUZZLIN'

Put your brain into gear and see how quickly you can solve these fun Little Mix puzzles.

WHICH WORD?

Complete these song titles by using the words from the list below.

1. Always be ...Together...

2. These ...Four... Walls

3. A Different ...Beat...

4. Black ...Magic...

 Beat

FIND THE PHONE

Noooooo! Leigh-Anne has lost her mobile! Which route should she take to find it?

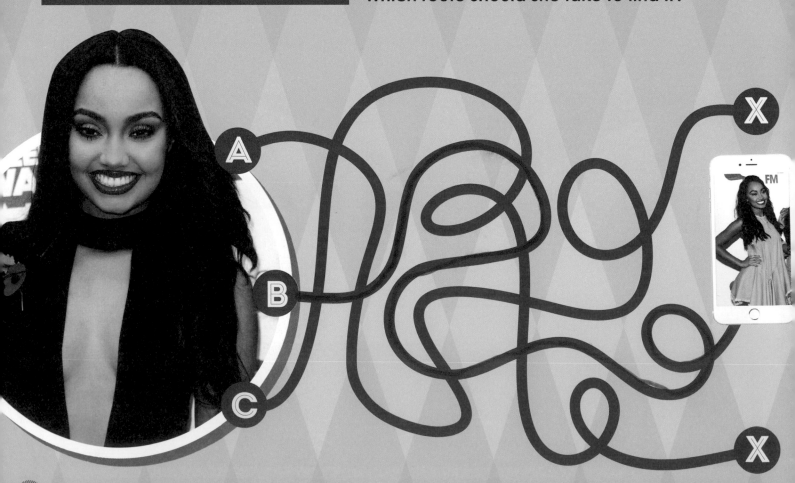

16

WHO'S HIDING?

Which Little Mix members are in disguise?

SHADY LADY

Which shadow matches this picture of Perrie exactly?

A   B   C

ANSWERS ON PAGE 76

10 BIG REASONS TO ♥

There are many reason why Little Mix rock. Here are 10 of the best…

1 WHAT YOU SEE IS WHAT YOU GET

Despite being huge celebs the girls are still down to earth. There are no pretences with these four.

2 THEY GENUINELY LOVE THEIR FANS

They know they wouldn't be where they are today without their fans and love the letters and scrapbooks they get sent from their Little Mixers.

3 THEY AREN'T AFRAID TO TALK ABOUT THE TOUGH STUFF

Jesy has talked about being bullied at school and Jade has opened up about anorexia. These brave girls don't pretend that everything in life is rosy.

4 THEY WORKED HARD TO MAKE IT

Even before *The X Factor* the girls spent years individually working towards their dreams – and they didn't give up when things got tough.

5 THEY DON'T TAKE THEMSELVES TOO SERIOUSLY

They wear fun clothes, they tease each other and they laugh – a LOT! The Little Mixes know how to enjoy life.

LITTLE MIX

6 THEY ARE SUPER TALENTED

Each girl is a great singer in her own right and together they are awesome!

7 THEY ARE EACH OTHER'S BFFS

They clicked when they first met and now the girls couldn't live without each other. Their friendship shines through in everything they do.

8 THEY EMBRACE THEIR INDIVIDUALITY

Although they're part of a group, the girls each have their own unique look and style. It's good to be one-of-a-kind!'

9 THEY HAVEN'T FORGOTTEN THEIR ROOTS

The Little Mixes still make time so see their friends and family and like doing 'normal' stuff like shopping and eating out.

10 THEY LOVE WHAT THEY DO

Perrie, Jesy, Leigh-Anne and Jade are doing what they've always dreamed of and it's obvious to everyone that they're having the time of their lives.

LITTLE MIX
fashion

From rocking the red carpet to performing on stage, the Little Mix girls always manage to look fabulous.

Jade looks sophisticated in a simple floor length dress and long gloves. The thigh high split adds a touch of cheekiness!

Jesy looks super cool in her oversized hoody. The fishnet tights and boots glam up the laid-back look.

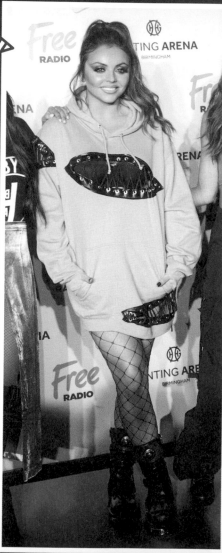

Leigh-Anne has teamed a cool slogan sweatshirt with eye-catching thigh-high boots. The perfect outfit for a photocall!

Little Mix prove you can never have too much denim in these super-cute outfits.

Perrie pulls off 70s style with these awesome black flares.

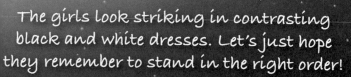

The girls look striking in contrasting black and white dresses. Let's just hope they remember to stand in the right order!

GET THE
LITTLE MIX *look*

1: Add funky accessories to every outfit.

2: Chill out in sweats and Lycra.

3: Team glam items with comfy casuals.

4: Layer up your outfits.

5: Embrace the high-top.

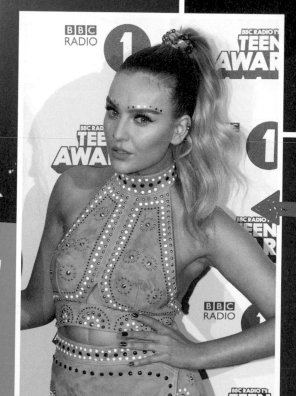

Perrie has totally gone for it in this studded halter neck dress. Her eyebrow bling completes the boho look.

planet
LITTLE MIX

Can you fit the words below into the grid? A few letters have been added to get you started.

FRIENDSHIP **SINGLES** **SONG** **FANS** **STAR**
ATTITUDE **ALBUM** **CELEB** **STYLE** **TELLY** **SWAGGER**

papped!

The girls have been snapped by the paparazzi! Work out where each piece fits to finish the pic.

ANSWERS ON PAGE 76

who are YOU?

My bedroom is always tidy. ✗

I prefer the natural look. ✓

I love being the centre of attention. ✓

It takes me ages to do my hair. ✗

I won't leave the house without my eyeliner. ✓

I'm always running late. ✗

My bedroom is full of teddies. ✓

I stick up for my friends. ✓

I'm not afraid to say it like it is. ✗

I've always got a smile on my face. ✓

I'm forever listening to music. ✓

I love sleeping. ✓

Which Little Mix member are you like? Tick the five statements that sound most like you to find out!

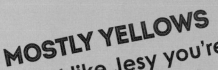

MOSTLY YELLOWS
Just like Jesy you're cool, funny and a little bit crazy! You two would have so much fun together!

MOSTLY PURPLES
You're quiet and thoughtful and always look out for your friends. You are so Jade!

MOSTLY PINKS
You're fun and bubbly and always keep your mates amused. You and Perrie are so alike you could be twins!

MOSTLY BLUES
You're passionate and independent, just like Leigh-Anne. You love your busy lifestyle but never get anywhere on time!

Friends come to me with their problems. ✗

I love wearing hats. ✗

I don't care what others think about me. ✓

I'm totally chilled out. ✓

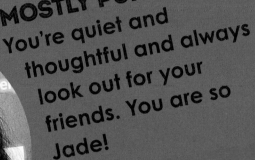

**A MIX OF COLOURS**
You're a complete mix of Little Mix – lucky you!

25

wardrobe
MALFUNCTION!

Disaster! Jesy's high heel has snapped!
Lead her through the maze to find her
trusty trainers to wear instead.

start

finish

MYSTERY MEMBER

Can you work out which one of Little Mix is being described below?

She comes from South Shields.

Beyoncé is one of her music icons.

Her favourite comfort food is curry.

Her birthday is in July.

Her celeb crush is Johnny Depp.

Perrie

She is the youngest in the band.

She describes her style as rocky and boho.

THE MYSTERY MEMBER IS...

....

ANSWERS ON PAGE 76-77

10 SECOND CHALLENGE

Look at this picture for 10 seconds then cover it up and see if you can answer the questions below.

1. How many TV screens are behind the girls?

2. Who is wearing a belt with their outfit?

3. What are the girls holding?

4. Is Jade wearing a dress or trousers?

5. How many of the girls have their hair down?

6. Which member is standing on the far right?

7. How many rings are on Jesy's fingers?

8. Are all the girls smiling?

9. Is anyone wearing a watch?

10. Does Perrie's dress have long or short sleeves?

NOW TRY THIS ON YOUR BFF!

extreme

Check out these
Little Mix close-ups.
Can you work out
who they all are?

1

4

7

2

5

3

6
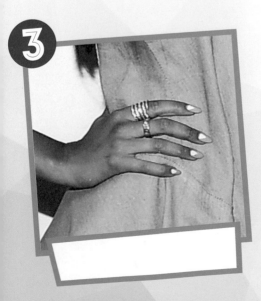

8

ANSWERS ON
PAGE 76-77

CHECK THE facts

Want to know more about Little Mix? Then read on to discover if these statements about the popsters are true or false.

Little Mix originally had a different name.

TRUE!

When the girls were first put into a band on The X Factor they were called Rhythmix. They changed to Little Mix after discovering there was a charity already using the Rhythmix name.

The girls all lived together before they won The X Factor.

TRUE!

All four Little Mixes moved into Perrie's family home between Boot Camp and Judges' Houses so they'd have lots of time to rehearse.

Before Little Mix Jade had already competed in X Factor Live Shows as a solo singer.

FALSE!

Although Jade had auditioned for The X Factor in previous years she'd only ever got as far as Boot Camp and had never made it to the Live Shows.

In 2016 Little Mix's Get Weird Tour became the UK's highest selling arena tour.

TRUE!

SOLD OUT SOLD OUT SOLD OUT

Little Mix were in high demand and sold over 300,000 tickets in 34 arenas across the UK.

SOLD OUT SOLD OUT SOLD OUT

As a child Jesy starred in the film Man on Fire opposite Denzel Washington.

FALSE!

Jesy auditioned for the film and got down to the final four but in the end the part went to Dakota Fanning.

Perrie bought her mum a house.

TRUE!

After finding fame with Little Mix generous Perrie splashed out on a pad for her proud mam.

33

PUZZLE MANIA!

Have fun solving these Little Mix tricky teasers.

MIX IT UP

How many words can you make from the letters in LITTLE MIX? Write your answers below.

Little Mix

1. ....
2. ....
3. ....
4. ....
5. ....

6. ....
7. ....
8. ....
9. ....
10. ....

HOW DID YOU DO?

0-2 words: Not bad!

3-5 words: Great job!

5+ words: Awesome!

CELEB SEQUENCES

Look carefully at the sequences below. Can you work out which of the Little Mixes completes each one?

IN PIECES

Uh oh, Jade has smashed her phone screen! Can you piece the broken parts of this picture back together?

ANSWERS ON PAGE 76-77

what's your POPSTAR STYLE?

If you were a singing celeb like the Little Mixes how would you roll?

Where would you rather shop?

A) A high street store

B) A designer boutique

What's your idea of a great night in?

A) Watching a movie in my PJs with my BFF

B) Pampering myself with a manicure and facial

How would you rather travel?

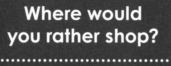

A) The bus is fine

B) Call me a cab, please

How do you spend your birthday money?

A) On lots of little things so it goes further

B) On one big expensive item

What sort of food do you prefer?

A) Hearty home-cooked meals

B) Fancy finger food

How long do you spend doing your hair?

A) I just brush and go

B) As long as it takes to get it just right

Mostly As - Girl-next-door
You appreciate the simple things in life. Even if you were a superstar you'd still have your feet firmly on the ground, just like the Little Mixes.

Mostly Bs - Popstar Diva
You like the finer things in life. If you were a popstar you'd make the most of it and enjoy all the celebrity trimmings. You only live once after all!

SECRET message

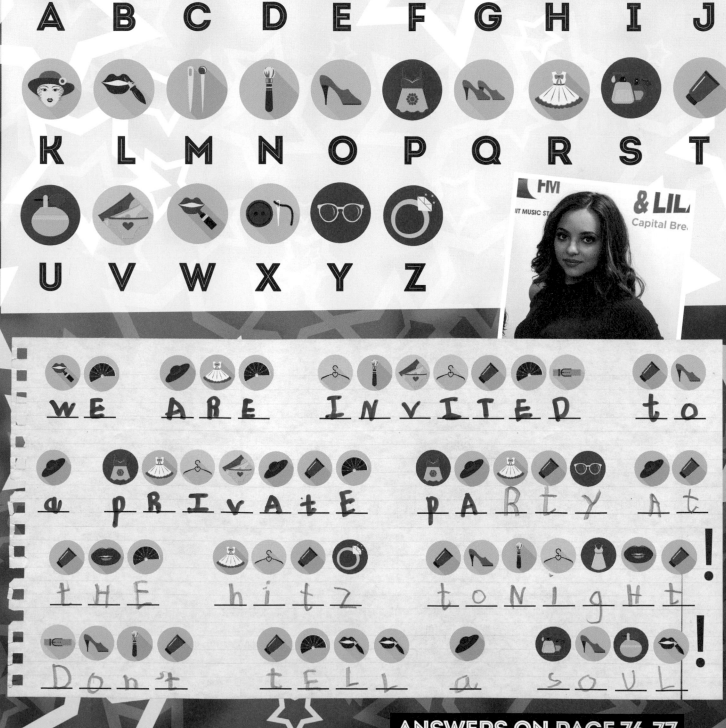

WE ARE INVITED to
a PRIVATE PARTY at
tHE hitz tonight!
Dont tELL a soUL!

ANSWERS ON PAGE 76-77

37

RULES FOR LIFE

When it comes to living a fulfilled life, the Little Mixes know a thing or two. Why not take a leaf from their rulebook?

BELIEVE IN YOURSELF

Back in the days before Little Mix, when the girls were trying to find fame as solo singers, they had their fair share of knockbacks. But if they hadn't believed in themselves, even through the tough times, Little Mix wouldn't be here today (imagine that!).

SEEK ADVICE FROM THOSE WHO KNOW YOU BEST

When you have a problem who better to talk to than the people who know you best. The Little Mixes are always there for each other and they have the support of their families too. A problem shared is a problem halved and all that.

DON'T LISTEN TO GOSSIP

Nobody likes to hear horrible things said about them but Jesy, Jade, Perrie and Leigh-Anne learnt early on that it's just not worth wasting time worrying about what other people are saying. Whether it's a rumour in the press or a whisper in the playground, if it ain't true then just ignore it!

EAT A LITTLE OF WHAT YOU FANCY

Since being in Little Mix the girls have had a strict diet and exercise regime but they still like to treat themselves to from time to time. In fact, Jesy's favourite meal is Nando's quarter chicken with lemon and herbs, chips and rice. Mmmmmm!

LOOK OUT FOR YOUR FRIENDS

Jesy, Perrie, Jade and Leigh-Anne are a tightknit gang who have each other's backs. They're protective, supportive and are always there for each other. What more could you ask from a BFF!

WEAR WHAT YOU WANT

The Little Mixes aren't afraid to wear what they like, even if it isn't strictly following fashion. Although they are in a group, they each have their own unique look and style rather than being carbon copies of each other. And as long as they like it, it doesn't matter what anyone else thinks!

LOVE WHO YOU ARE

Even celebs have their insecurities but If you are happy with who you are then your confidence will shine through. Jesy has been known to say that you should never try to be anyone other than you – if everyone was the same the world would be a boring place!

WORK HARD FOR WHAT YOU WANT

From the day they were first put together, Little Mix worked hard to earn their place in *The X Factor* final. And even after being crowned the winners the girls didn't slow down. They are troopers with unfaltering ambition and bags of enthusiasm and all that hard work has certainly paid off!

LITTLE MIX A-Z

Because they're a whole alphabet worth of awesome!

 IS FOR AUDITIONS
It was third time lucky for Jade with *The X Factor*.

 IS FOR *BLACK MAGIC*
The catchy tune reignited the group's career after a long break.

 IS FOR CAPRICORN
Jade's star sign.

 IS FOR DOWN-TO-EARTH
They might be celebs but they're keeping it real!

 IS FOR ELOCUTION LESSONS
Jesy had these at stage school and lost her Essex twang.

 IS FOR FATE
The girls believe it's what brought them together.

 IS FOR *GET WEIRD*
The album got to number 2 and the tour was a sell-out.

 IS FOR HIGH WYCOMBE
Leigh-Anne's home town.

 IS FOR INDIVIDUAL
These girls are most definitely one-of-a-kind!

 IS FOR JAPAN
Perrie's all-time favourite country.

IS FOR KELLY ROWLAND

The *X Factor* judge who asked the girls if they could work together as a group.

IS FOR LITTLE MUFFINS

The cute nickname that Little Mix's mentor, Tulisa, gave the band.

M IS FOR MACHINE GUN KELLY

The superstar rapper featured on the remix of *No More Sad Songs*.

IS FOR NEW NAME

The group changed its name from Rhythmix halfway through *The X Factor*.

IS FOR O2

Little Mix performed at this humungous arena on their *Get Weird Tour*.

IS FOR PUBLIC EYE

These days the girls are never out of it!

IS FOR QUEUING

At the start of their X Factor journey the girls queued for hours to audition.

IS FOR ROMFORD

The Essex town that Jesy calls home.

IS FOR SOUTH SHIELDS

Jade and Perrie both hail from here.

IS FOR TALENT

The girls have oodles of it!

IS FOR UNIQUE

Each Little Mix member has her own individual sound, look and style.

IS FOR VIDEOS

The girls' fun videos have seen them line dancing, dressed as geeks and working out at the gym.

IS FOR WAITRESS

Leigh-Anne's job before pop stardom beckoned.

IS FOR *THE X FACTOR*

The show that shot the girls to fame.

IS FOR YOU!

The girls know that they wouldn't be anything without their fans.

IS FOR ZARA

Apparently Jade's favourite high street store.

SONG SEARCH

Find all the Little Mix songs hidden in this wordsearch.

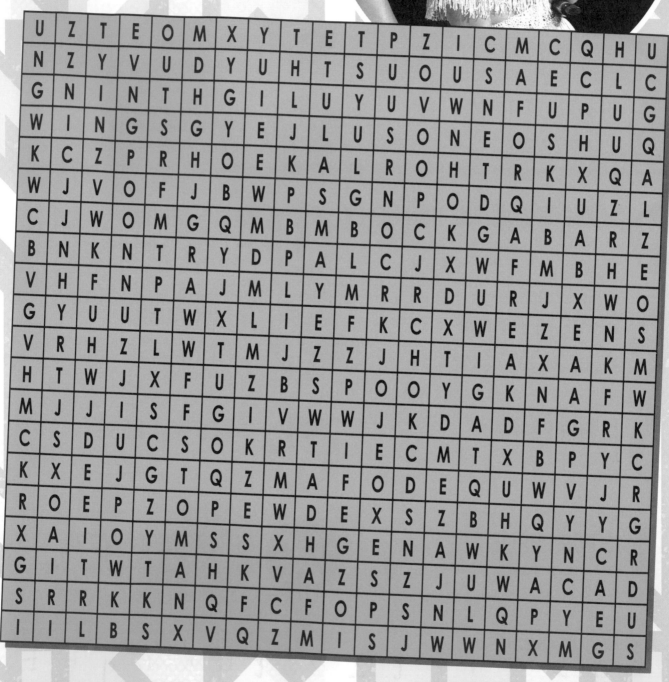

U	Z	T	E	O	M	X	Y	T	E	T	P	Z	I	C	M	C	Q	H	U
N	Z	Y	V	U	D	Y	U	H	T	S	U	O	U	S	A	E	C	L	C
G	N	I	N	T	H	G	I	L	U	Y	U	W	N	F	U	P	U	G
W	I	N	G	S	G	Y	E	J	L	U	S	O	N	E	O	S	H	U	Q
K	C	Z	P	R	H	O	E	K	A	L	R	O	H	T	R	K	X	Q	A
W	J	V	O	F	J	B	W	P	S	G	N	P	O	D	Q	I	U	Z	L
C	J	W	O	M	G	Q	M	B	M	B	O	C	K	G	A	B	A	R	Z
B	N	K	N	T	R	Y	D	P	A	L	C	J	X	W	F	M	B	H	E
V	H	F	N	P	A	J	M	L	Y	M	R	R	D	U	R	J	X	W	O
G	Y	U	U	T	W	X	L	I	E	F	K	C	X	W	E	Z	E	N	S
V	R	H	Z	L	W	T	M	J	Z	Z	J	H	T	I	A	X	A	K	M
H	T	W	J	X	F	U	Z	B	S	P	O	O	Y	G	K	N	A	F	W
M	J	J	I	S	F	G	I	V	W	W	J	K	D	A	D	F	G	R	K
C	S	E	D	U	C	S	O	K	R	T	I	E	C	M	T	X	B	P	Y	C
K	X	E	J	G	T	Q	Z	M	A	F	O	D	E	Q	U	W	V	J	R
R	O	E	P	Z	O	P	E	W	D	E	X	S	Z	B	H	Q	Y	Y	G
X	A	I	O	Y	M	S	S	X	H	G	E	N	A	W	K	Y	N	C	R
G	I	T	W	T	A	H	K	V	A	Z	S	Z	J	U	W	A	C	A	D
S	R	R	K	K	N	Q	F	C	F	O	P	S	N	L	Q	P	Y	E	U
I	I	L	B	S	X	V	Q	Z	M	I	S	J	W	W	N	X	M	G	S

SALUTE TOUCH **WINGS** BOY **POWER** LIGHTNING

CANNONBALL FREAK **GROWN** OOPS

MADHOUSE **DNA** HAIR **OMG**

IMPOSTER PIC

These six pics may look the same but one is slightly different to the rest. Can you spot the odd one out?

A

B

C

D

E

F

ANSWERS ON PAGE 76-77

45

what's your POPSTAR JOB?

Imagine if you were in Little Mix's entourage!
Find out what your dream job would be.

DOES PERFORMING ROCK YOUR WORLD?

NO →

DO YOU ADORE HITTING THE HIGH STREET?

YES ↓ (from Does performing rock your world?)

NO ↓ (from Do you adore hitting the high street?)

ARE YOU SUPER ORGANISED?

NO → **DO YOU ACCESSORISE EVERY OUTFIT?**

YES ↓ (from Are you super organised?)

YES ↗

NO ↓ (from Do you accessorise every outfit?)

ARE YOU ALWAYS FIRST ON THE DANCEFLOOR?

NO → **ARE YOU ALWAYS ON TIME?**

46

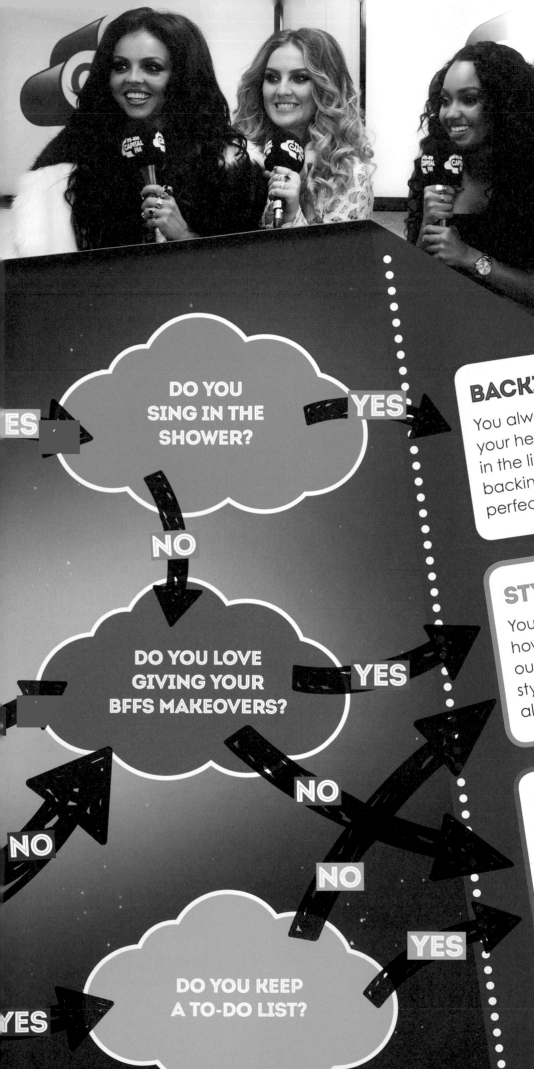

DO YOU SING IN THE SHOWER?

YES

NO

DO YOU LOVE GIVING YOUR BFFS MAKEOVERS?

YES

NO

NO

YES

NO

YES

DO YOU KEEP A TO-DO LIST?

YES

BACKING SINGER

You always have a song in your head and love being in the lime light. Little Mix's backing singer would be the perfect job for you!

STYLIST

You love shopping and know how to accessorise any outfit. You would be the girls' stylist and make sure they always looked fabulous!

MANAGER

You love planning things and would never turn up late ... for anything! Your dream job would be as the group's superstar manager!

SCRAMBLED SONGS

Oh no, the song titles on Little Mix's playlist have been mixed up! Can you unscramble each one and write the correct title in the space below it?

1. on remo das gsons

5. toush tuo ot ym xe

2. tiltle em

6. aoutb hte ybo

3. who ay iodn'?

7. peeb ebpe

8. baklc gimac

4. velo em ro elaev em

48

POPSTAR SUDOKU

Sudoku puzzles are Jade's favourite! Have a go at this Little Mix one to see what all the fuss is about!

<table>
<tr><td></td><td></td><td></td><td></td></tr>
<tr><td> Perrie</td><td></td><td></td><td></td></tr>
<tr><td>Leigh-Anne</td><td></td><td></td><td></td></tr>
<tr><td></td><td></td><td></td><td></td></tr>
</table>

RULES

Write the girls' names in the right squares to complete the puzzle. Each Little Mix member can only appear once in each row, column and box.

Jesy

Perrie

Leigh-Anne

Jade

ANSWERS ON PAGE 76-77

49

next GLAMOUR

51

missing
PIECES

Woo hoo, Little Mix are celebrating another number 1! Which NINE jigsaw pieces complete this picture?

A ....

B ....

C ....

D ....

E 1 ....

G ....

H 2 ....

I ....

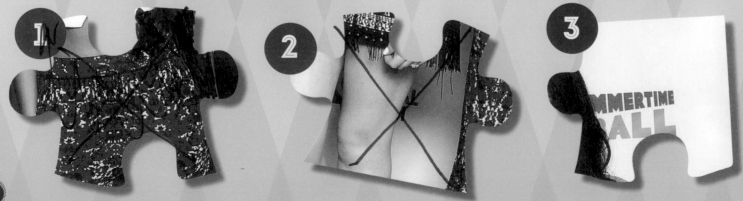

1

2

3

ANSWERS ON PAGES 76-77

SEEING *double*

Leigh-Anne, Jesy, Jade and Perrie are out and about.
Can you spot **15 differences** between these colourful
Little Mix pictures?

ANSWERS ON PAGE 76-77

my LITTLE MIX!

This section is all about Little Mix and you! Fill it in and keep it forever.

MY FAVOURITE MEMBER IS...

Jesyika .

I AM LITTLE MIX'S BIGGEST FAN BECAUSE...

They are very pretty and Sing good Songs.

THE BEST SINGER IS...

Jesyika

THE FIRST LITTLE MIX SONG I BOUGHT WAS...

THE MOST AWESOME DANCER IS...

Jesyika

THE COOLEST DRESSER IS...

Jesyika .

THE BEST LITTLE MIX VIDEO IS...

power .

THE ONE WITH THE GREATEST HAIR IS...

Jesyike.

MY FAVOURITE LITTLE MIX ALBUM IS...

power

THE MEMBER I WOULD MOST LIKE TO LOOK LIKE IS...

Tesyike

ONE THING I HAVE IN COMMON WITH LITTLE MIX IS...

They are so pretty

IF I EVER MET THE GIRLS I WOULD...

Skrem!

little
LOVES

Japan
It's Perrie's favourite country in the world. She loves the wacky feel of the place, the culture and, of course, the shopping!

Liquid eyeliner
Jade doesn't like leaving the house without it!

Tattoos
Jesy loves them, even though she's scared of needles! She's got tons including the date in Roman numerals that the girls got together.

Curry
Perrie loves it so much that sometimes she even eats it for breakfast!

Nachos
Piled high with soured cream, salsa and cheese, they're Leigh-Anne's favourite comfort food.

TOWIE
Jesy's favourite way to chill out is by watching the Essex show in her PJs with no make-up and a pizza!

River Island
It's one of Leigh-Anne's favourite shops and the branch in her home town once opened up exclusively for her to shop!

Headbands
They're Perrie's favourite item of clothing and she's lost count of how many she owns.

Tea
Jade can't start the day without a nice cuppa.

mix

HATES

Putting the rubbish out
Perrie can't stand this whiffy chore!

Flying
Poor Jade is petrified of being in the air and tries to fall asleep before take-off.

Bags
But only if they're on the table when Leigh-Anne is about to eat! She prefers her dining area to be bag-free and who can blame her!

Opening night
Jade still struggles with stage fright on the first show of a tour but once she gets into the performance her nerves soon disappear.

Rollercoasters
Perrie has a fear of the big, stomach-churning rides.

Negative press
The girls have all been on the receiving end of nasty comments in the press and on social media. At first it used to really affect them but now they just ignore it.

Greasy food
Jesy finds it hard when the girls are stateside because even the salads in America seem to come smothered with oil!

Spiders
Perrie and Jesy are both terrified of the eight-legged creepy crawlies.

Flying insects
Wasps, moths, daddy-long-legs, Leigh-Anne hates them all!

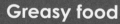

SHHH! IT'S A SECRET!

Here are some things you might not know about your favourite girl group.

Leigh-Anne has a celeb crush on Justin Bieber! She loves his music and clean cut look.

Perrie has no sense of smell!

Jesy would love Little Mix to cover a Spice Girls song – their own version of course!

Jesy was an extra in the film Harry Potter and the Goblet of Fire. Look out for her in the ballroom scene!

Jesy is obsessed with trainers and owns about 400 pairs!

One of Jesy's nicknames is Whining Willow because she enjoys having a good old moan!

Jade loves drawing and painting – she's really good at it too!

Perrie loves teddies and has been known to carry a soft toy around with her!

Leigh-Anne is a talented songwriter.

Jade is scared of clowns.

Perrie's a bit of a softie! Sad films have her in tears and when she's tired she'll cry at anything!

When she was younger Jesy was a champion sprinter but gave up because the sound of the starting gun scared her!

Perrie is a little bit crafty! She loves making things and knows how to knit.

Jade loves doing puzzles – especially sudoku.

Apparently Jade never burps! Like never! Not even once in her whole entire life!

LITTLE MIX

MATCH

How quickly can you match these popstar pictures into pairs?

A

B

C

D

E

F

ANSWERS ON PAGES 76-77

THE THREE PAIRS ARE...

DESIGN A DRESS

Lucky Leigh-Anne is off to a premiere but she need a new frock. Be a super stylist and design a dress for her to wear.

Don't forget to accessorise!
Draw some shoes, a bag and some jewellery to go with your design

SHOES

BAG

JEWELLERY

PUZZLE mania

NAME GAME

Cross out the letters that appear twice then rearrange the ones that are left to reveal the middle name that two of Little Mix share.

R K A D E M I

J T O R L T J

A S U K M D

THE NAME IS...

...Lily...........................

IN A BLUR

Uh-oh, this selfie is out of focus! Can you work out which Little Mix member it is?

....

WHOSE HAIR?

Can you recognise which barnet belongs to which member?

1  **2**  **3**  **4**

1
....

2
....

3
....

4
....

ANSWERS ON PAGES 76-77

LITTLE MIX *hair*

Up, down, curly or straight, Little Mix aren't afraid to experiment with their hairstyles.

Perrie's fishtail plait manages to look cool and sophisticated at the same time.

Leigh-Anne's tight curls and Perrie's poker straight locks look great side-by-side.

Leigh-Anne looks super-cute with her hair pulled back into a spiky bun.

Not everyone can get away with such a harsh style but Perrie pulls off the scraped-back high ponytail to perfection.

Jesy always looks best with big hair and this sweeping side fringe really suits her.

GET THE
LITTLE MIX *look*

1. Don't be afraid to experiment with wild colours - if in doubt use a spray in colour that will wash out easily.

2. Accessorise with clips, bows or headscarves.

3. When going for waves or curls, think big.

4. Use serum and hair straighteners to get a super sleek look.

5. Try out lots of different hairdos to discover what works for you.

Jade rocks the 'girl next door' look with natural looking, loose waves.

TOP SECRET TEXTS

Jade and Perrie are making plans. Use the key to decipher their text messages and find out what they're up to!

CODE

★ = E

❀ = S

✌ = B

☎ = A

Little Mix

W★ n★★d ☎ d☎y off! L★t'❀ h★☎d to th★ ✌★☎ch.

I'm in! W☎nna go in di❀gui❀★ ☎nd t☎k★ th★ ✌u❀?

Y★☎h, th☎t would b★ fun!

☎w★❀om★! M★★t you ☎t th★ ✌u❀ ❀t☎tion ☎t 10☎m.

❀ure thing. I'll b★ th★ on★ in th★ Mick★y Mou❀★ m☎❀k!

Hmmm, not r★☎lly wh☎t I h☎d in mind wh★n I ❀☎id di❀gui❀★!

Think it might dr☎w too much ☎tt★ntion?

Just ☎ ✌it!

How ☎bout hug★ ❀ungl☎❀❀★❀ ☎nd ☎ floppy h☎t?

P★rf★ct! ❀★★ you ❀oon.

ANSWERS ON PAGE 76-77

HOW BIG A FAN ARE YOU?

Take this fun quiz and all will be revealed!

1. How many times have you seen the band?:
a) None yet but I can't wait to see them live.

b) At least one concert.

c) I haven't missed a tour yet.

2. When you hear *Black Magic* do you:
a) Hum along quietly.

b) Join in with the chorus.

c) Belt out every single word as loud as you can.

3. How many Little Mix albums do you own?
a) None but I have all my favourite singles.

b) At least one and I'll be buying their next one.

c) Every single one – in at least one format.

4. When you see a magazine with Little Mix on the cover do you:
a) Read the coverlines to decide if it's worth buying.

b) Have a quick flick through to see what's inside.

c) Buy the mag as quickly as you can before it sells out.

5. Jesy says plimsolls are the new high-tops, Do you:
a) Browse plimsolls online.

b) Try a pair on to see if they suit you.

c) Rush out and purchase two pairs in your favourite colours.

Mostly As - Quiet Fan
You love the Little Mixes but don't feel the need to shout it from the rooftops. You're happy to follow from afar, listening to your fave tracks, reading about the girls in magazines and tuning in when they're on TV.

Mostly Bs - Mega Fan
You're a huge Little Mix fan and know oodles about the girls. You like to sing along to all their classics and are first on the dancefloor when a Little Mix tune comes on.

Mostly Cs - Super Fan
You live and breathe Little Mix! You never miss a TV appearance and every lyric to every song is etched on your brain forever. What you don't know about the Mixes isn't worth knowing!

IMAGE ID

Only one of the small pictures is identical to the big image of Leigh-Anne. Can you spot which it is?

A

B

C

D

72

IT'S showtime!

ANSWERS ON PAGE 76-77

You've got front row tickets to see Little Mix and the show is about to start! Make your way through the maze to the arena as quickly as you can.

START

ARENA

THE GREAT BIG
LITTE MIX *quiz*

How well do you know your favourite girl group? Answer these quiz questions to find out!

Question 1

Jade is the youngest member of the group.

TRUE ☐   FALSE ☐

Question 2

Little Mix won *The X Factor* in 2012.

TRUE ☐   FALSE ☐

Question 3

Japan is Perrie's favourite country

TRUE ☐   FALSE ☐

Question 5

Rapper Machine Gun Kelly features on *No More Sad Songs*.

TRUE ☐   FALSE ☐

Question 4

Jesy's Roman numeral tattoo shows her date of birth.

TRUE ☐   FALSE ☐

Question 6

Perrie and Leigh-Anne are both from South Shields.

TRUE ☐ FALSE ☐

Question 7

Wings was the group's first number 1.

TRUE ☐ FALSE ☐

Question 8

Leigh-Anne was working as a waitress before Little Mix.

TRUE ☐ FALSE ☐

Question 9

Jesy owns over 400 pairs of earrings.

TRUE ☐ FALSE ☐

Question 10

Leanne's celebrity crush is Justin Bieber.

TRUE ☐ FALSE ☐

HOW WELL DID YOU DO?

0-3 CORRECT	4-7 CORRECT	8-10 CORRECT
UH-OH, FAIL!	NOT BAD AT ALL!	GOLD STAR FOR YOU!

ANSWERS ON PAGE 76-77

ANSWERS

Page 16-17:
Which Words?
1. Together
2. Four
3. Beat
4. Magic

Find the Phone
Route B

Who's Hiding?
Jesy and Jade

Shady Lady
B

Page 22-23:
Planet Little Mix

Papped!
1E, 2D, 3B, 4C, 5F, 6A

Page 26:
Wardrobe Malfunction!

Page 27:
Mystery Member
Perrie

Page 28:
10 second challenge
1. Two,
2. Jesy,
3. Microphones
4. Dress
5. All of them
6. Jade
7. Seven
8. Yes
9. Yes, Leigh-Anne
10. Long sleeves

Page 29:
Extreme Close-up
1. Perrie
2. Jesy
3. Leigh-Anne
4. Leigh-Anne
5. Perrie
6. Jade
7. Jade
8. Jesy

Page 34-35:
Celeb Sequences
1.    2.

3.    4.

In Pieces
1C, 2D, 3A, 4H, 5G, 6J

Page 37:
Sercet messge
WE ARE INVITED TO A PRIVATE PARTY AT THE RITZ TONIGHT! DON'T TELL A SOUL!

Page 44:
Song Search

Page 45:
Imposter Pic
Picture E

Page 48-49:
Scrambled Songs

1. No More Sad Songs
2. Little Me
3. How Ya Doin'?
4. Love Me or Leave Me
5. Shout Out to My Ex
6. About the Boy
7. Beep Beep
8. Black Magic

Popstar Sudoku

Page 52-53:
Missing Pieces

A 4, B 9, C 7, D 13, E 1, F 6,
G 17, H 2, I 12

Page 54-55:
Seeing Double

Page 64:
Little Mix Match

Picture A matches F
Picture B matches E
Picture C matches D

Page 66-67:
Name Game

Louise – both Jesy and Perrie have this middle name.

In a Blur

Jade

Whose Hair?

1. Jesy
2. Perrie
3. Jade
4. Leigh-Anne

Page 70-71:
Top Secret Texts

We need a day off! Let's head to the beach.

I'm in! Wanna go in disguise and take the bus?

Yeah, that would be fun!

Awesome! Meet you at the bus station at 10am.

Sure thing. I'll be the one in the Mickey Mouse mask!

Hmmm, not really what I had in mind when I said disguise!

Think it might draw too much attention?

Just a bit!

How about huge sunglasses and a floppy hat?

Perfect! See you soon.

Page 72-73:
Image ID

Picture B is identical

It's Showtime!

Page 74-75:
The Great Big Little Mix Quiz

1. False – Perrie is the youngest.
2. False – Little Mix won *The X Factor* in 2011.
3. True.
4. False – Jesy's tattoo shows the date the girls first got together.
5. True.
6. False – Perrie and Jade are both from South Shields.
7. False – Cannonball was the group's first number 1.
8. True.
9. False – Jesy wons over 400 pairs of trainers.
10. True.

PICTURE CREDITS

Cover:

Doug Peters/EMPICS Entertainment

Ian West/PA Wire/PA Images

Back cover:

Chris J. Ratcliffe/PA Wire

Content:

2-3:   Ian West/PA Archive/PA Images

4-5:   Doug Peters/EMPICS Entertainment

6-7:   Ian West/PA Archive/PA Images,
           Owen Humphreys/PA Archive/PA Images

8-9:   Doug Peters/EMPICS Entertainment,
           Yui Mok/PA Archive/PA Images, Matt
           Crossick/Empics Entertainment

10-11:   Daniel Leal-Olivas/PA Archive/PA Images,
          Matt Crossick/Empics Entertainment

12-13:   Daniel Leal-Olivas/PA Archive/PA Images,
          Doug Peters/EMPICS Entertainment

14-15:   Ian West/PA Archive/PA Images,
          Daniel Leal-Olivas/PA Archive/PA Images,
          Doug Peters/EMPICS Entertainment

16-17:   Ian West/PA Archive/PA Images, Doug
          Peters/EMPICS Entertainment

18-19:   Ian West/PA Wire/PA Images

20-21:   Doug Peters/EMPICS Entertainment,
          Katja Ogrin/EMPICS Entertainment,
          Daniel Leal-Olivas/PA Archive/PA Images,
          Matt Crossick/Empics Entertainment,
          Ian West/PA Wire/PA Images

22-23:   Meleah Loya/AFF/PA Images,
          Yui Mok/PA Archive/PA Images

24-25:   Ian West/PA Archive/PA Images

26-27:   Doug Peters/ EMPICS Entertainments

28-29:   Daniel Leal-Olivas/PA Archive/PA Images,
          Ian West/PA Archive/PA Images

30-31:   John Phillips/EMPICS Entertainment

32-33:   Ian West/PA Archive/PA Images,
          Roberto Finizio/Zuma Press/PA Images,
          Daniel Leal-Olivas/PA Archive/PA Images,
          Doug PetersEMPICS Entertainment

34-35:   Ian West/PA Wire/PA Images,
          Suzan Moore/EMPICS Entertainment

36-37:   John Phillips/EMPICS Entertainment,
          Ryan Phillips/PA Archive/PA Images

38-39:   Ian West/PA Archive/PA Images.
          Ryan Phillips/PA Archive/PA Images,
          John Phillips/EMPICS Entertainment

40-41:   Dominic Lipinski/PA Wire/PA Images

42-43:   John Barrett/Zuma Press/PA Images,
          Suzan Moore/EMPICS Entertainment

44-45:   Yui Mok/PA Archive/PA Images,
          Doug Peters/EMPICS Entertainment

46-47:   Daniel Leal-Olivas/PA Archive/PA Images

48-49:   Ryan Phillips/PA Wire.
          Ian West/PA Archive/PA Images

50-51:   Doug Peters/EMPICS Entertainment,
          Chris J. Ratcliffe/PA Wire,
          Ian West/PA Wire, Matt Crossick/ EMPICS
          Entertainment, Danny Lawson/PA Wire,
          Matt Crossick/ EMPICS Entertainment

52-53:   Ian West/PA Archive/PA Images

54-55:   Ian West/PA Archive/PA Images

56-57:   Dominic Lipinski/PA Wire/PA Images,
          Ian West/PA Archive/PA Images

58-59:   Ian West/PA Wire/PA Images,
          Doug Peters/ EMPICS Entertainment.

60-61:   gotpap/Starmax/PA Images

62-63:   Ian West/PA Archive/PA Images

64-65:   Lexie Appleby/Geisler-Fotopress/DPA/PA
          Images, Owen Humphreys/PA Archive/PA
          Images

66-67:   Demis Maryannakis/Starmax/PA Images,
          Doug Peters/ EMPICS Entertainment

68-69:   Ian West/PA Wire, gotpap/Starmax/PA
          Images

70-71:   Meleah Loya/AFF/PA Images,
          Ian West/PA Archive/PA Images

72-73:   Ryan Phillips/PA Archive/PA Images,
          Doug Peters/Doug Peters/EMPICS
          Entertainment

74-75:   Ryan Phillips/PA Archive/PA Images, Doug
          PetersEMPICS Entertainment, AJM/EMPICS
          Entertainment, Daniel Leal-Olivas/PA
          Archive/PA Images, Matt Crossick/ EMPICS
          Entertainment

76-77:   Suzan Moore/EMPICS Entertainment,
          DOUG PETERS/ EMPICS Entertainment, Ian
          West/PA Archive/PA Images

LIVING THINGS

PLANT PARTS

BY

STEFFI CAVELL-CLARKE

©2017
Book Life
King's Lynn
Norfolk PE30 4LS

ISBN: 978-1-78637-076-1

All rights reserved
Printed in Malaysia

A catalogue record for this book
is available from the British Library.

Written by:
Steffi Cavell-Clarke

Edited by:
Grace Jones

Designed by:
Drue Rintoul

CONTENTS

Words that look like **this** can be found in the glossary on page 24.

WHAT IS A PLANT?

Planet Earth is home to many living things. All living things need water, air and sunlight to grow and survive. Plants, animals and humans are all living things.

A DOG IS A LIVING THING.

A SUNFLOWER IS A LIVING THING.

A BOOK IS A NON-LIVING THING.

Trees, shrubs, herbs, grasses, ferns and mosses are all different types of plant that can be found on planet Earth. Some plants have flowering parts and others do not. Even though plants may look different from one another, many still share the same parts.

PLANT PARTS

Most flowering plants have roots, a stem, leaves and flower heads. Each of these plant parts has a **function** that helps to keep the plant alive and healthy.

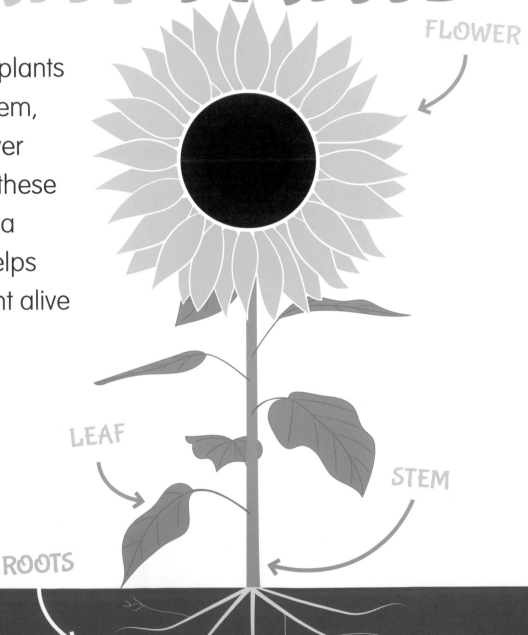

FLOWER

LEAF

STEM

ROOTS

6

Leaves make food for the plant.

Roots hold the plant in the ground and **absorb** water and **nutrients** from the soil.

The stem holds the plant up.

Flower heads produce **pollen** and seeds.

SEED

New plants grow from seeds. Many seeds are blown away from plants by the wind and usually become buried in the soil. For a seed to grow, it needs water from the rain and warmth from the sun. Once it has enough water and warmth it will start to **germinate**.

8

Seeds come in all different shapes and sizes. For example, poppy seeds are very small, whilst the horse chestnut tree produces big seeds which have spiky green shells around them.

HORSE CHESTNUT SEEDS

SUNFLOWER SEEDS

POPPY SEEDS

ROOTS

As the seed splits open, a root begins to grow downwards from the seed. The roots have important functions that help the plant to grow. One of the functions of the roots is to absorb water and nutrients from the soil.

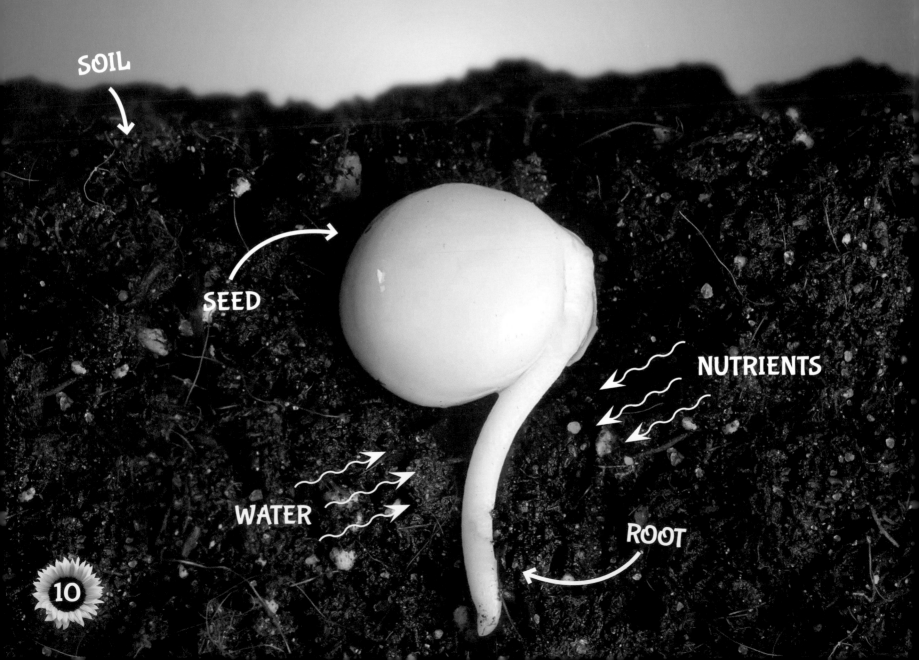

SOIL

SEED

NUTRIENTS

WATER

ROOT

As the plant grows, extra roots develop in order to absorb more water and nutrients. Most roots grow underneath the surface of the soil and **anchor** the plant to the ground. This provides a strong base, which helps to stop the plant from blowing away in the wind.

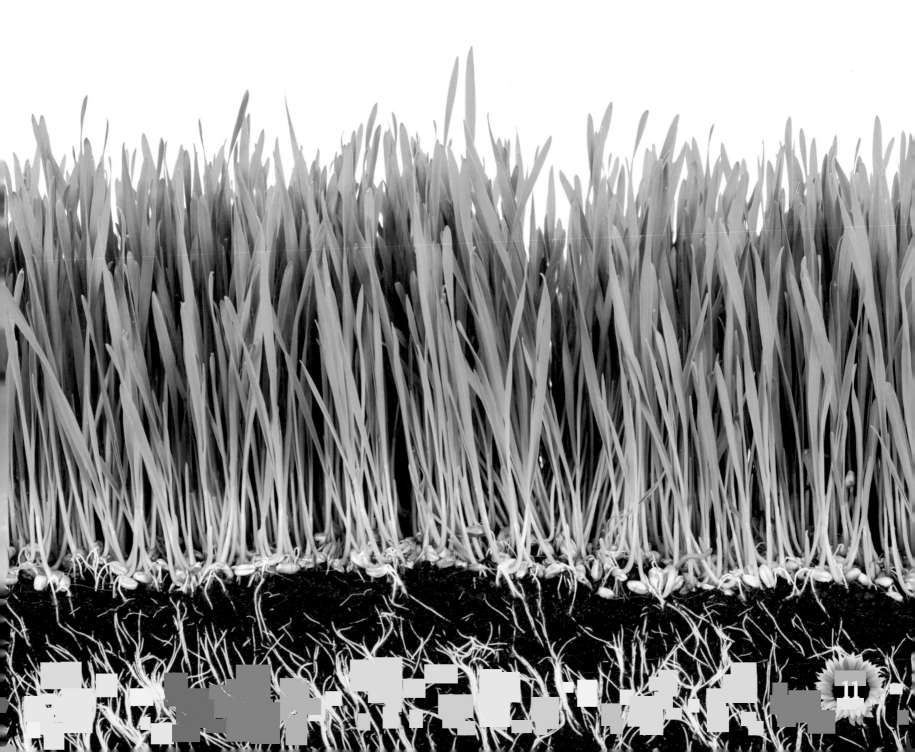

SHOOTS

Out of a seed grows a tiny shoot. This is called a seedling and it sprouts through the soil upwards towards the sunlight. The seedling is the first plant part that grows towards the sun. The light from the sun gives the new plant the **energy** it needs to grow.

SUN

SEEDLING

SOIL

ROOTS

12

As the seedling continues to grow, it will develop more shoots that will begin to produce leaves and flowers.

SHOOT

THE GROWING STAGES OF A SEEDLING

STEM

The seedling develops into a stem as it continues to grow above the soil. The stem supports the whole plant and holds the leaves up to the sun so they can absorb as much sunlight as possible.

STEM

The stem connects the roots to the other plant parts. It **transports** water and nutrients from the roots to all the other parts of the plant, such as the leaves. Without the stem, the plant would not be able to survive.

NUTRIENTS

WATER

LEAVES

As the plant grows, it will start to develop leaves. Leaves grow from shoots that branch out from the stem. The function of a leaf is to make food for a plant, which it needs in order to survive.

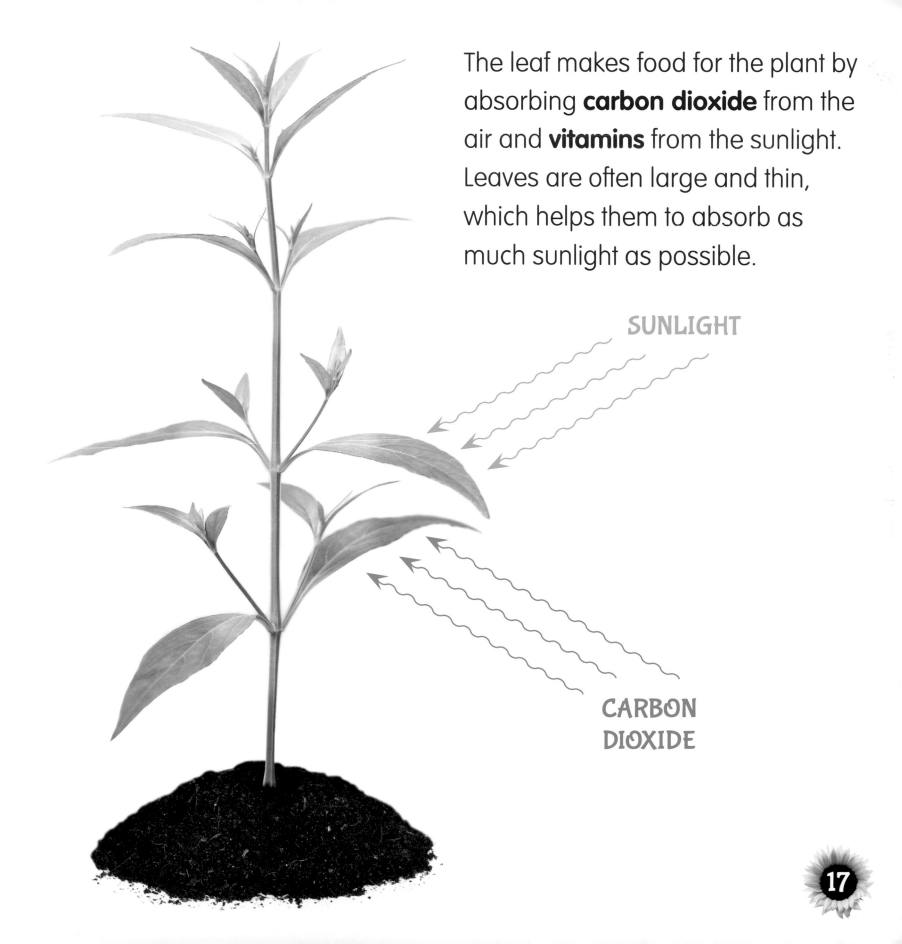

The leaf makes food for the plant by absorbing **carbon dioxide** from the air and **vitamins** from the sunlight. Leaves are often large and thin, which helps them to absorb as much sunlight as possible.

SUNLIGHT

CARBON DIOXIDE

FLOWER

Many plants grow one or more flower heads. A flower starts as a small bud that grows from a shoot and opens up into a flower head. The flower head has lots of different parts and some of them produce pollen and seeds.

PETAL

STAMEN

The petals around the flower head protect the delicate plant parts inside, like the stamen. The stamen produces pollen for the plant, which is used to make new seeds. The seeds can be blown away from a plant by the wind.

SEEDS

NOT ALL FLOWERS HAVE PETALS.

TREES

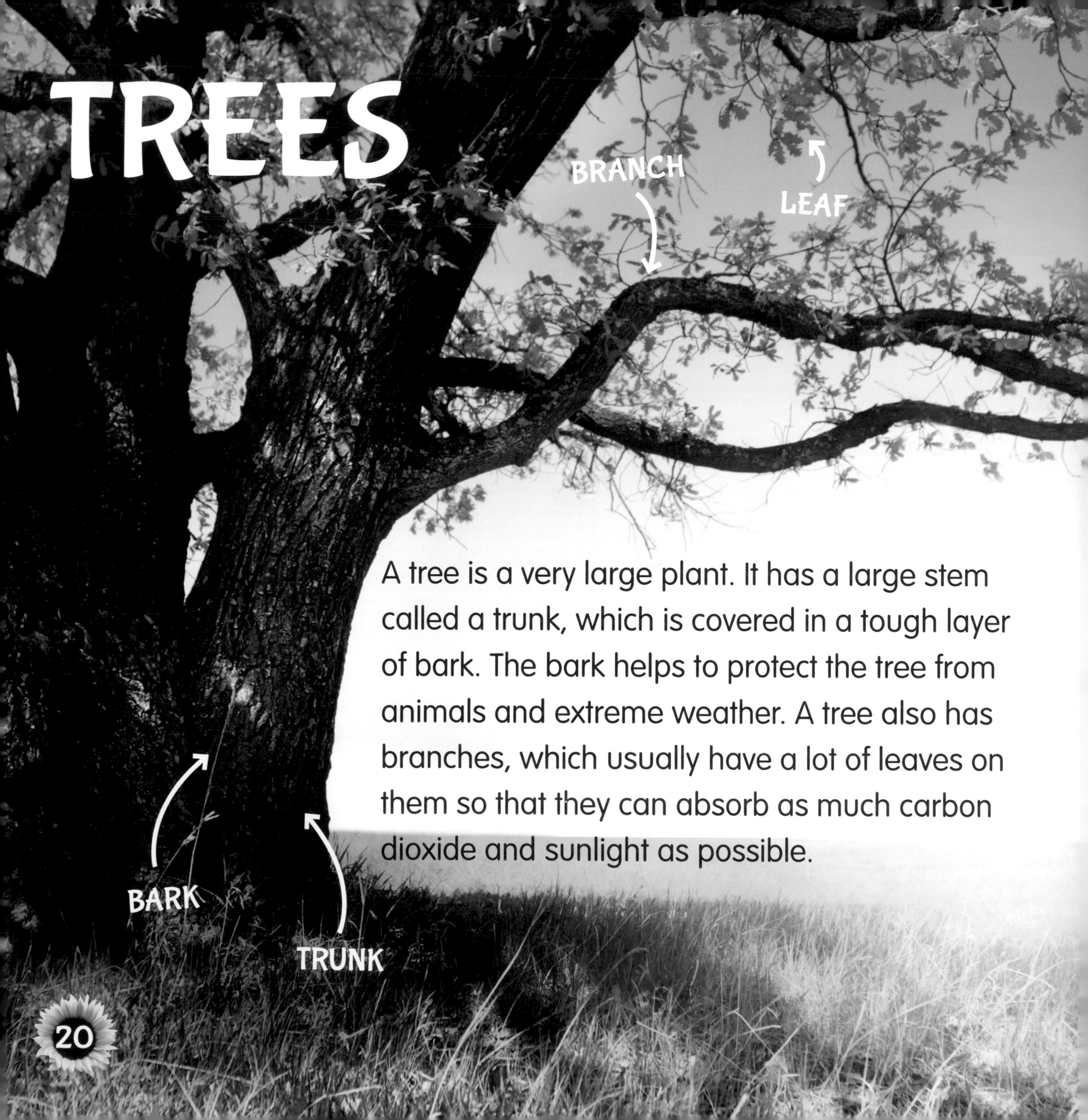

BRANCH

LEAF

A tree is a very large plant. It has a large stem called a trunk, which is covered in a tough layer of bark. The bark helps to protect the tree from animals and extreme weather. A tree also has branches, which usually have a lot of leaves on them so that they can absorb as much carbon dioxide and sunlight as possible.

BARK

TRUNK

Very large trees tend to have thick roots to anchor the plant upright into the soil. Larger trees need to absorb more water and nutrients than smaller trees.

WATER

NUTRIENTS

LET'S EXPERIMENT!

Do you know what seeds need to grow?
Let's find out!

You will need:

TOP TIP
- - - - - - -
ASK AN ADULT TO HELP YOU!

TWO CLEAN, SHALLOW TRAYS

PAPER TOWELS

CRESS SEEDS

WATER

22

Step 1

Place a thick layer of paper towels in the bottom of each tray. Label the trays A and B. Wet the paper towels in tray A.

Step 2

Put tray A in a warm room next to a window.

Step 3

Place tray B in the fridge, so it has no warmth or light.

Step 4

After 5 days, some of seeds will have started to grow. Which tray did the seeds grow in and can you see how they are different?

TOP TIP

MAKE SURE THAT YOU ADD A LITTLE WATER TO TRAY A, TO KEEP THE SEEDS MOIST.

Results:
Your experiment will show you that seeds need light, warmth and water to grow. If they do not have all of these, they will not grow into healthy plants.

23

GLOSSARY

absorb soak something up
anchor a heavy weight that holds something down
carbon dioxide colourless gas found in the air
energy the ability to do a job
function a specific action
germinate when a seed begins to grow
nutrients substances for growth and health
pollen yellow dust found in flower heads
transports moves something from one place to another
vitamins substances needed for normal and healthy growth

INDEX

This
Lit
w\
libı